On the Ball

Learning to Identify the Place Values of Ones and Tens

Autumn Leigh

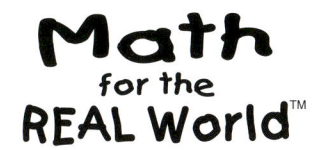

Math for the REAL World™

Rosen Classroom Books & Materials
New York

Let's count groups of ten in a sports store.

We see ten soccer balls. That is one group of ten.

tens **1** ones **0**

10 soccer balls

We see eleven baseballs.

That is one group of ten and one baseball left over.

tens **1** ones **1**

11 baseballs

We see twelve footballs.

That is one group of ten and two footballs left over.

tens **1** ones **2**

12 footballs

Words to Know

10	11	12
ten	eleven	twelve

baseball football  soccer ball